THE MASTER'S PIECE

by *Precious Gem*

WESTBOW
PRESS®
A DIVISION OF THOMAS NELSON
& ZONDERVAN

WestBow Press books may be ordered through booksellers or by contacting:

WestBow Press
A Division of Thomas Nelson & Zondervan
1663 Liberty Drive
Bloomington, IN 47403
www.westbowpress.com
1 (866) 928-1240

ISBN: 978-1-9736-7758-1 (sc)
ISBN: 978-1-9736-7759-8 (hc)
ISBN: 978-1-9736-7757-4 (e)

Library of Congress Control Number: 2019916419

Print information available on the last page.

WestBow Press rev. date: 10/23/2019

I would like to dedicate this book to my loving husband Samuel, whose love and leadership has helped me birth my gift of writing. Your gentle love and godly leadership are daily reminders of how precious I am in God's eyes. I also dedicate this book to my loving son Jeremiah, who has been my joy since he entered the Earth. Special thanks and acknowledgement to my loving church family at Church of Lord who prayed for and supported me through my worst of times. Lastly, I want to dedicate this book to my dear sister in Christ and friend Jazz who always held me accountable with constant reminders to keep writing.

CONTENTS

INTRODUCTION

This is the word that came to Jeremiah from the Lord: go down to the potter's house, and there I will give you my message. So, I went down to the potter's house, and I saw him working at the wheel. But the pot he was shaping from the clay was marred in his hands; so, the potter formed it into another pot, shaping it as seemed best to him. Then the word of the Lord came to me.

—Jeremiah 18:1–5 (NIV)

This passage was written in the days of Jeremiah the prophet. It was written to the nation of Judah, which had gained for itself a reputation of forgetting God. The people of Judah, who had once known and walked with God, now found themselves in a position where they had left their first love in exchange for foreign gods and idolatrous practices. Throughout the scope of this prophecy, across a span of forty years, Judah experienced nothing but chaos throughout the land, corruption in government, declining morality, evil infecting the people, and more. How did the nation get to such a devastated place? What happened along the way? When did the shifting away from God and everything pertaining to godliness began?

You may have already guessed it: the garden of Eden. This is essentially where everything and everyone began. In the garden were the hands that formed the soil that created a man, whose rib was used to form a woman, whose body was given the assignment to birth a child. "Whose hands?" you ask. The hands of the Potter, the Master, the Creator, God Himself. It is He who has made us and not we ourselves (Psalm 100:3). Without Him, nothing was made that was made (John 1:3). However, to really grasp this truth, we must go to the beginning to get an account of how it all began.

"In the beginning God created the heavens and the earth. Now the earth was formless and empty, darkness was over the surface of the deep, and the Spirit of God was hovering over the waters" (Genesis 1:1–2 NIV). In other words, the Earth was as a lump of clay without a shape and assigned purpose. The opening verses of the Bible give us an astounding affirmation of God's existence and His creative ability. There was no room left for imagination here; the stage was set, and God was on the move displaying His opening performance. On days one through three, He gave form to the Earth and on days four through six, He filled it. This proved God to be the Potter of all potters. He is the original designer for everything that is good and perfect. He holds the pattern for everything. He is the architect of the universe. God is the maker of heaven and Earth. He is the manufacturer of life. Every plant, animal, human being, and aspect of nature is derived from God.

A potter is the creator that makes an object out of a lump of clay. The potter does this by molding the clay with his or her hands and mind to create a form in space. In the process, from raw clay to a finished product, the shaped form is decorated and made ready to display the masterpiece. This is precisely what God did with the Earth. After He assessed the condition of the lumped clay of Earth, He decided that it was just what He needed to create His masterpiece of human beings. As clay in the potter's hands, God subjected the Earth to six days of dividing, gathering, planting, and filling before He reached His final product. The Bible records that it wasn't until after God created Adam and Eve on the sixth day that He rested on the seventh day. God couldn't rest until His work of art was completed.

How did God create humankind? What process did he employ? Well, much like a potter, He formed and then filled. The Bible records that "God formed man from the dust of the ground and breathed into his nostrils the breath of life, and man became a living being" (Genesis 2:7 NIV). The Hebrew word for *man* is pronounced *aw-dawm*, from which *Adam* is derived. It's also related to *aw-dawm-ah*, which means red earth, or red clay, indicating the natural earth elements that composed Adam's body and the body of every human being since.

> So the Lord God caused the man to fall into a deep sleep; and while he was sleeping, he took one of the man's ribs and then closed up the place with flesh. Then the Lord God made a woman from the rib he had taken out of the man, and he brought her to the man. The man said, this is now bone of my bones and flesh of my flesh; she shall be called 'woman,' for she was taken out of man. That is why a man leaves his father and mother and is united to his wife, and they become one flesh. (Genesis 2:21–24 NIV)

In other words, God took a piece of clay from Adam, stretched it, and formed Eve to ensure that they were "one." Eve's original name, when translated, meant simply "woman," (a "female man") just as Adam was known simply as "man" (a "male man"). Later, Adam prophetically named his wife Eve because she would become the mother of all the living (Genesis 3:20). Eve is derived from the Hebrew word that means "life-giving."

Although God took less than one day to create Adam and Eve, on average the time it takes to create pottery is said to be over three weeks. In His omnipotence and omniscience, God is the exception to every rule. He is the Master, and

He defied time and created Adam and Eve in the record-breaking time of one day! There is absolutely nothing too hard for God. He stands outside of time and brings forth possibility where there is none by adding His "super" to our natural. We truly serve an awesome God, and my goal is to inspire you through the pages of this book to enlarge your view of God. I believe that as you see God for who He is (i.e., the Master of everything), you will in turn see yourself for you were created to be (i.e., the Master's piece).

CHAPTER 1
Test for a Testimony

Do not be afraid; you will not be put to
shame. Do not fear disgrace; you will not be
humiliated. You will forget the shame of your
youth and remember no more the reproach
of your widowhood.

—Isaiah 54:4 (NIV)

This is the verse that God would bring to my attention
every time I was haunted by the ugliness of my past. I
will take the time now to elaborate on what this verse meant
to me. I grew up in a single-parent household as the only
female and the youngest of five. Life for me was hard, to say
the least. At a very young age, I experienced a great deal of
pain and endured abuse of all kinds. I was sexually molested,
physically and verbally abused. I had a fragmented childhood.

I was forced to not have any friends and was followed to
school, beaten, threatened, and monitored daily to ensure
my silence. I was impregnated twice and forced to secretly
abort both pregnancies by my most frequent abuser. One

can imagine the horror of the pain that accompanied such experiences. Of course, out of fear that I would be killed by my abusers if I ever exposed them, I never told anyone of the horrid abuse I endured daily for most of my adolescent years. I cried more times than I thought was humanly possible. I could not comprehend why I had been through so much pain and violence. I thought, *Why me? What did I do to deserve all this pain? When will it ever end?* This abuse caused me to spend many years feeling unloved, ugly, rejected, wounded, and ashamed.

I kept thinking, *What man would want to be with me after I have been molested so many times that I lost count?* I convinced myself that God did not love me, and neither would the man of my dreams. The cycle of pain continued until I was about fourteen, when I decided to confess to the police most of what was happening to me. It was on this day that my most frequent abuser told me that it would be my last day on earth. He threatened me and was very determined to kill me that day. As he chased me through a five-story apartment building in Brooklyn, pinned me up against a glass window, and attempted to throw me out of it, my whole life flashed before my eyes. I couldn't believe my life was about to end that way. I was so young; I hadn't accomplished any of my dreams.

By some divine intervention, he could not open the window; it was jammed shut. At the same time, a resident of the building came running to the scene, and an argument arose between this man and my abuser. This distraction gave me enough time to run from the scene and flee to safety. As I hid beneath the first-floor staircase, my heart was pounding, my clothing was torn, and my hair was disheveled. I knew in my heart that escape was now or never. I remained silently under the staircase until I could hear that he had left the building. I could hear him speeding away in his car in the hopes of finding me on the street.

Moments later, I knocked on the door of an apartment on the ground floor of the building and met the residents to whom I eventually told my story. They comforted me and called the cops on my behalf. As I was placed under police custody, I reported all the abuse I had endured by my worst abuser, but I did not have the courage to report the others.

Following this incident, a legal determination was made to take me away from home. Consequently, I spent some time in a group home, followed by a foster home. As I lived in the home of this lovely Hispanic woman in the Bronx, some amazing things happened to me. By far the most memorable was being given my first pocket-size New Testament Bible. It was the first time I could remember feeling hopeful that my life would change for the better. I had never met the God of this Bible, but I had heard enough about Him to know that He could change my life.

Immediately following the foster home experience, I was ordered by the court to live with my godmother. It was the best alternative option to being home. My godmother happened to be a God-fearing woman. She was a devoted Christian along with her husband, who saw to it that I regularly went to church. We attended prayer meetings on Monday and Tuesday nights, Bible study on Wednesday nights, and an 8:00 a.m. service on Sunday mornings. With her loving support and guidance, I soon found myself on my knees at a Tuesday night prayer meeting, devoting my life to Jesus. It was September 11, 1998. Some months following that night, I was baptized and became a member of the church she attended.

My godmother taught me how to pray, serve, and love. She was truly a blessed role model—one that I had never prayed for but that God knew I needed. Soon after my conversion, the courts gave me clearance to return home. Shortly after my return home, my loving godmother passed away from cancer. I was devastated because I had never even realized she was sick. She had always been so full of life and energy. I realized that I must have been her last assignment on earth.

She seemed to pass so suddenly after mentoring and loving me back to some state of normalcy. I believe she is now in the arms of the Lord and that I will one day be reunited with her in eternity. As I had come to believe it would, my life was about to drastically change for the better. I became very involved in my church, joining the choir, dance team, usher board, and more. I developed a passion for the Bible and rigorously studied it. Academically, I progressed and went on to graduate both high school and college with honors. I was sure that the next major step in my life was meeting my Prince Charming and having a happy ending.

I could not have been more wrong. Although I thought I had met this person and that my painful cycle of abuse had ended, it resurfaced in the worst way. My only solace during this time was the birth of my son, whom I like to refer to as my bundle of joy. The days when I wanted to end my life or wallow in despair were circumvented by the beautiful gift of my son. I knew that I had to live for him. One look into his eyes kept me from losing my mind. Somehow, God used him to give me constant reminders that I was loved and that everything would be all right.

In the years to come, I endured more physical, emotional, and mental abuse. I was crushed. No one could prepare me for the storm I was about to face. Over the next five years, I moved at least six times. With little to no money, I struggled for years as a single parent, living with family members and friends until I was finally able to settle down and purchase my own home.

Along the way, I had received many offers from men who were trying hard to court me and win me over with their charm. Due to my fear of reliving the painful relationship with my son's father, I was hesitant to accept their offers. However, against my better judgment, several years later I yielded to the offer of another man who appeared to be very spiritual and charming in the beginning. He convinced me that he would love me and treat me better than I had ever experienced. This made me feel safe, so I proceeded to date him, only to find out that he was an even worse abuser. We had gotten to the point of engagement when I was faced with being smacked, punched, thrown against glass, called foul names, and—worst of all—being falsely accused on the Internet and in the community of fornicating with him. The man turned out to be my worst nightmare. My son had to witness the beatings and the abuse; my heart was broken again. Once I was able to get free from that man, I vowed to never go through that again.

Years went by, and God restored me as He promised He would. In due time, I went back to school and finished my master's coursework, and I am now a few courses away from obtaining my doctorate degree. I became very involved in ministry and discovered my passion to pray, teach, and lead.

While doing ministry, I eventually met my current husband. Through him, I was able to experience the love of God in a way I had never known before. Today we are happily married and are living the life we both dreamed of. I started my own business and have answered the calling on my life to be an author. God took the pain of my past and used it to birth my purpose. Without my painful experiences, there would not be a book to write. You hold this book in your hand today because God had my life in His hands the whole time. God knew all along that although the devil meant evil and harm for me, He would turn it around for my good. He is the Master who knows how to create masterpieces from the many strokes of life. Life can be hard, but God is always good! My trial was for a testimony, and so is yours. Be encouraged, and know that the worst is over and the best is yet to come.

CHAPTER 2

Honor God

You are worthy, our Lord and God, to receive
glory and honor and power, for you created
all things, and by your will they were created
and have their being.

—Revelation 4:10–11 (NIV)

The essence of what it means to honor God is revealed
to us in what Jesus called the first and greatest
commandment: "love the Lord your God with all your
heart and with all your soul and with all your mind. This
is the first and greatest commandment" (Matthew 22:37–
38 NIV). This scripture clearly implies that God wants to
have first place in our lives. As the Creator of our lives, He
honestly deserves it. The daily effort that we make to place
God at the top of our list of priorities is a sure indication that
we honor Him. Honor means to show respect and esteem
to an individual. Oftentimes the degree to which honor
is bestowed on someone is directly correlated with the
person's position and achievements. Furthermore, honor

can be depicted through various attitudes, affections, and actions.

More specifically, common attitudes associated with honor include regard, respect, and reverence. The affections we experience toward those we honor include admiration, adoration, or even awe. The actions we take toward those who we honor include praise, submission, and obedience. For example, children honor their parents through their submission and obedience. Consequently, when we honor God, we regard Him with respect, reverence, admiration, adoration, awe, praise, submission, and obedience. It is vital for to us realize that honoring God should never be limited to religious external rituals or ceremonies. To honor God in the way Jesus encouraged us to in Matthew 22, God must be involved into every fabric of our lives.

Whether it be in our careers, marriage, ministry, or parenting, God must be included into every facet. One clear way to do so is pray and ask for His guidance and direction prior to making major decisions. Jesus gave us many wonderful examples of how to do this throughout His time on Earth. We saw Him rise early in the morning to pray, isolate Himself for prayer and fasting, and pray for God's blessing and direction while ministering. Spiritual disciplines such as prayer, Bible reading, worship, and service are key components of the Christian faith, but they also lend themselves to means by which we can honor God. Prayer, for example, gives us an opportunity to acknowledge God as the source of all our needs and the answer to all our problems. As we cry out to God in prayer, He promises to answer us and deliver us from all our troubles (Psalm 91:15). Much like parents desire that their children approach them with all their needs, so our heavenly Father desires to hear from His children with their hurts, fears, concerns, dreams, problems, and basic need for conversation. The following verses are few of the many we can find in the Bible that highlight the importance of prayer in our lives.

> This is the confidence we have in approaching God: that if we ask anything according to his will, he hears us. And if we know that he hears us whatever we ask we know that we have what we asked of him. (1 John 5:14–15 NIV)

> And I will do whatever you ask in my name, so that the Son may bring glory to the Father. You may ask me for anything in my name, and I will do it. (John 14:13–14 NIV)

> Do not be anxious about anything, but in everything, by prayer and petition, with thanksgiving, present your requests to God. And the peace of God, which transcends all understanding, will guard your hearts and

your minds in Christ Jesus. (Philippians
4:6–7 NIV)

We can all attest to the fact that almost every major
purchase we make from the store is accompanied by a
manual that informs us how to get the most out of our
purchase. The manual usually exists as a guide on how to
use, protect, and care for the product we purchased. These
manuals are written by manufacturers primarily because
they are designed to reveal the gadget's original purpose
and function. The Bible works in the same exact way.

The scriptures are like an operation manual for human
life, and God's words help us learn, through the lives of
others, how to navigate life as the Creator intended. Much
like the gadgets we purchase, the Bible teaches us how to
use, protect, and care for our lives. When we don't make a
habit of reading the Bible, we are like a ship without a sail.
We risk living a life without clear meaning, direction, and
purpose. What use is it to have a great product or tool yet
not know how to use it to its fullest potential? You guessed
it: it defeats the purpose of having it at all. God created us
all for a specific purpose that only He, as the manufacturer
of our lives, can reveal to us when we are ready to receive
the revelation through the study of scriptures.

In the same way prayer and Bible reading are significant,
worship is a Christian imperative if we are aiming to be like
Christ. Jesus emphasizes that true worshippers are precisely
whom the Father is seeking: "But the hour is coming, and

now is, when the true worshipers will worship the Father in spirit and truth; for the Father is seeking such to worship Him. God is Spirit, and those who worship Him must worship in spirit and truth" (John 4:23–24 NIV). When we worship the Lord, we should do so with intention and reverence.

When we worship the Lord, we should focus on Him as the Supreme Being, not to mention the one to whom all honor is due. When Jesus defeated Satan in the wilderness by resisting his offer to bow down and worship him (Matthew 4:10), He clearly depicted the heart of a true worshipper. Worship extends beyond affection and has more to do with the acknowledgment of God's invaluable worth and merit as the one whom we place above all else.

Service is yet another activity that we can do to demonstrate our love for God. For Christians, service is not merely a means for them to give back to society; it is also the heartbeat and pulse of our call to discipleship. Throughout the course of Jesus's life on earth, He had a remarkable commitment to serve others that we as His disciples are called to emulate. Our willingness to serve is an indication that we are maturing in spiritual virtues as well as determined to love God through people. "For even the Son of Man did not come to be served, but to serve, and to give his life as a ransom for many" (Mark 10:45 NIV). Jesus came down to Earth with the primary assignment to demonstrate the love of God toward us sinners by giving His life as a ransom for many. The least we can do in return to show how much we love Him is to dedicate a portion of our lives to the service of others.

DISHONOR THROUGH DISOBEDIENCE

Nevertheless, despite our passionate attempts to demonstrate our love and honor for God, the Bible informs us that we all fall short of the ability to truly give God glory due to our sinful nature (Romans 3:23). Our sins are not only blatant violations of God's laws but also direct assaults on His honor (Psalm 51:4). When we choose to deliberately transgress the laws of God, whether we realize it or not, we are simultaneously dishonoring God.

But thanks be to God. Because of His great love for us, He sent Jesus Christ, who honored God through His perfect love, humility, and obedience as an example for us to follow. It is important to note that our heavenly Father informs us that we cannot honor Him unless we honor His Son, Jesus Christ. "Moreover, the Father judges no one, but has entrusted all judgment to the Son, that all may honor the Son just as they honor the Father. Whoever does not honor the Son does not honor the Father, who sent him" (John 5:22–23 NIV). Therefore, it is impossible for us to honor God unless and until we receive Jesus Christ as our Lord and Savior. It is only through faith in Jesus Christ that God removes the penalty our sins deserve and credits us with the honor and holiness of Christ's righteous life. "For the wages of sin is death; but the gift of God is eternal life through Jesus Christ our Lord" (Romans 6:23 NIV).

As a general principle, honor is an essential key to receiving answered prayers and blessings from heaven. Those who honor God will be honored. That's the way it works. Throughout the Bible, we see that all who honored Jesus received from God in the proportion to which the honor was rendered. This principle is clearly depicted in the story of Jesus at the house of Simon the leper. While Jesus was reclining at a table, a woman approached Him with an alabaster box (flask) filled with costly spikenard oil. The price of this perfume was equivalent to one year's salary at the time. Yet after weeping to wash Jesus's feet with her tears, the woman dried them with her hair, broke open the spikenard, and poured it on His head. The woman honored Jesus by lavishly anointing Him with what cost her a great deal of money. This was truly a great act of honor—one that had not been mentioned even among His disciples.

Not everyone who was present rejoiced at this outpouring. "Some of those present were saying indignantly to one another, why this waste of perfume? It could have been sold for more than a year's wages and the money given to the poor. And they rebuked her harshly" (Mark 14:4–5 NIV). How unfortunate for those who made this statement; they had obviously missed the bigger picture. Here lay before them an opportunity to honor the God of heaven and Earth by honoring His Son, and they missed it—whereas the woman they criticized had taken advantage of it. She honored Jesus, and He in turn honored her, saying, "Truly I tell you, wherever the gospel is preached throughout the world, what she has done will also be told, in memory of her" (Mark 14:9 NIV).

Sometimes honor is expressed in ways to God that can seem small or foolish to others. However, I encourage you to be steadfast like the woman ignoring the voice of the critics and naysayers. Your Lord eagerly awaits to receive your honorable acts or service. Be ready for Him to bless and honor you in return. God always has more in store for us than we can imagine or anticipate. He doesn't require anything from us to bless us or love us; however, it a guaranteed promise that those who honor Him will receive a portion greater than their counterparts. He knows our hearts and is moved when we esteem Him. Today, be encouraged to lavish God with reverence and love, regardless of how it may look to those around you. Simply wait to see how He pours out His love in return!

CHAPTER 3
In Him We Live

For in Him we live and move and have our being.

—Acts 17:28 (NIV)

Contrary to popular belief, without God we are nothing. If you turn to Genesis 2:7, you'll note that it wasn't until God breathed into the nostrils of Adam that he became alive: "Then the LORD God formed a man[a] from the dust of the ground and breathed into his nostrils the breath of life, and the man became a living being" (NIV). God is the Author of life. Without the breath of life, which represents the Spirit of God, we are mere dust or substance from the Earth. God's sole purpose of transferring the breath of life into man was to give him life or make him a living soul. Adam could not exist with a mere body—he needed a soul, which in turn would make him a spiritual being who mirrored the image of God. "Then God said, let us make mankind in our image, in our likeness, so that they may rule over the fish in the sea and the birds in the sky, over the livestock and all the wild animals, and over all the creatures that move along the ground" (Genesis 1:26 NIV). This spiritual state would now allow humans the full capacity to fellowship, serve, and relate to God because "God is spirit" (John 4:24 NIV).

Nevertheless, there are many individuals who have convinced themselves that there is no God despite their inability to disprove the story of Creation. They reason in their hearts, "Even if God exists, I still have to pay my bills and go to work, so what do I have to do with God? What can He do for me?" Take for example Super Bowl Sunday. As I consider the amount of people who will fill a stadium, as well as the number of viewers on TV, for a mere football game, I wonder how many of these same people were in church that day. The answer is likely less than half because people have convinced themselves that either there is no God or He is not significant enough for them to acknowledge. This is a sad yet daunting truth. Much like to the dismay of any parent rejected by a child, I wonder how God feels about being rejected by His greatest work.

If you survey the lives of these same individuals, you will find no healthy fear of God. The Bible informs us that "The fear of the Lord is the beginning of wisdom, and knowledge of the Holy One is understanding" (Proverbs 9:10 NIV). This verse suggests that the fear of God is at the core of true wisdom, causing all other types of knowledge to be worthless unless built upon knowledge of the Lord Himself. Therefore, it is to our benefit to live our lives with the fear of God as a central theme. Without this resolved, we will ultimately be led to a dark place called deception.

The fear of the Lord essentially involves the continual awareness that our God is able to see and hold us accountable for every action committed, word spoken, or thought conjured. God knows everything, and there is nothing that escapes His attention. This is clearly depicted in Psalm 139:1–8 (NIV).

> You have searched me, Lord,
> and you know me.
> You know when I sit and when I rise;
> you perceive my thoughts from afar.
> You discern my going out and my lying down;
> you are familiar with all my ways.
> Before a word is on my tongue
> you, Lord, know it completely.
> You hem me in behind and before,
> and you lay your hand upon me.
> Such knowledge is too wonderful for me,
> too lofty for me to attain.
> Where can I go from your Spirit?
> Where can I flee from your presence?
> If I go up to the heavens, you are there;
> if I make my bed in the depths, you are there.

Like David, the author of Psalm 139, for us to maintain the fear of the Lord, we must acknowledge God for who He is. God must be revered as the Creator and heavenly Father. As we commit to having a continual awareness of our God, we become more apt to obey Him. The issue that presents itself most times, however, is our attempts to create our own image of God using earthly wisdom. In so doing, many people have created a God in their minds that is extremely tolerant of sin and lawlessness and will never hold them accountable for their actions.

This kind of a god that makes us feel comfortable is very permissive and exists solely to bless us and cater to our every whim. This deceptive depiction of God will always cause us not to fear Him in the way He deserves to be feared. The Lord our God is mighty and far greater than that. The fear of the Lord begins when we recognize Him in His majesty and power. "You are worthy, our Lord and God, to receive glory and honor and power, for you created all things, and by your will they were created and have their being" (Revelation 4:11 NIV).

Here's some food for thought: if some of us were more aware that God was watching us, how many of us would be more careful about what we do, say, and act? Think about it. Right now, in this moment where you are, there is an invisible camera zooming in on everything that you say, think, and do. My question to you is, Is God pleased with what He hears and sees, or is He grieved? Do we really care about what God thinks anymore, or have we become so accustomed to our own way of doing things that God's opinion is now irrelevant? Has the fact that there is a God who is to be revered been reduced to a mere theory and concept that is to be addressed only as needed?

The fact of the matter is God created everyone and everything! It is crucial that we grasp this concept because the number one lie that was ever told is that we can live without God. Satan seduced Adam and Eve and caused them to believe this huge lie in the garden of Eden from the beginning.

> "Now the serpent was more crafty than any of the wild animals the Lord God had made. He said to the woman, did God really say, you must not eat from any tree in the garden'? The woman said to the serpent, "We may eat fruit from the trees in the garden, but God did say, You must not eat fruit from the tree that is in the middle of the garden, and you must not touch it, or you will die. You will not certainly die, the serpent said to the woman. For God knows that when you eat from it your eyes will be opened, and you will be like God, knowing good and evil. When the woman saw that the fruit of the tree was good for food and pleasing to the eye, and also desirable for gaining wisdom, she took some and ate it. She also gave some to her husband, who was with her, and he ate it." (Genesis 3:1–6 NIV)

Satan deceptively convinced them that God didn't love them. His false evidence was the knowledge that he claimed God was keeping from them. However, the truth is God loved them dearly, so much so that He allowed them to choose Satan over Him by giving them free will. Although God in His omniscience knew that Adam and Eve would betray Him, He still allotted them the gift of free will. This is again a sign of true love. God never intended to force Himself unto Adam and Eve; He knew that true love will always draw others to itself, and it never has to force itself on anyone. It is important that we never mistake God being all-powerful with being controlling. God is love, and love is *not* controlling (1 John 4:8). Only Satan dares to control others because this attribute is rooted in fear. People control only what they fear. It makes sense that God wouldn't do so because "perfect love drives out fear" (1 John 4:18 NIV).

Satan was a liar from the beginning. "He was a murderer from the beginning, not holding to the truth, for there is no truth in him. When he lies, he speaks his native language, for he is a liar and the father of lies" (John 8:44). One of his greatest lies is that one can sin and get away with it, whereas the Bible clearly states that the wages of sin is death (Genesis 2:17; Romans 6:23). In the absence of the truth of God's Word and will, Eve was left with her natural and physical desires. The consequent result was immediate alienation from God and her spouse, Adam.

The lesson to learn here is that Satan's lies are just that, lies—they will never come to pass! Sin always comes to rob us of life and the blessings bestowed upon us by God. Adam and Eve ultimately were deceived to exchange life for death, pleasure for pain, abundance for lack, and fellowship for alienation. The painstaking result in the end of Satan's deception in the garden of Eden was what we know today as the fall of man. Where exactly did they fall from? They fell from a position of dominion, authority, power, and rule into one of shame and subjection to sin and the devil. Moreover, they lost the most precious possession ever known to humankind: the presence of God.

The lesson we learn through this story is that when the enemy comes in and makes you feel as though you can make decisions for your life outside of God's will, it is a lie and a trap. Like it did in the garden, it will lead to your downfall. Of course, the effects of their decision weren't apparent while looking at the fruit and desiring it to eat. If they knew what would come after they bit the fruit, they would have never eaten it. The trick of the devil remains the same. He offers us what is appealing to our senses (eyes, ears, touch, etc.), also known as flesh, and we never see the devastating effects to come after we succumb to the temptation. This is an alarming reminder for us to walk not according to the flesh but rather according to the Holy Spirit and every Word that proceeded out of the mouth of God! If God didn't say and confirm it, don't do it. I don't care how good it, he, or she looks—don't do it! Let's make up in our minds that we will not make a move without God!

Now, let's look at God's response to Adam and Eve's

disobedience. God's immediate response to them was one of grace and redemption. God Himself sacrificed an animal to make a "covering" for them because they were hiding out of the shame of their nakedness (Genesis 3:8; Genesis 3:21). The beauty of the text is that this animal was symbolic of Jesus Christ, who is the ultimate sacrifice and covering for all sin. God wanted humankind and the devil to know that He is God and always has a plan! There is no mess that He can't handle, nothing broken that He can't fix, nothing wounded that He can't heal, nothing dead that He can't resurrect. God is awesome!

By virtue of this covering that God provided for humankind in the garden of Eden, centuries later the prophecy was fulfilled at the cross. When Jesus died on the cross, He created a path of redemption back to our Eden status. His death took back what was lost in the garden (e.g., power, authority, rule, dominion). Jesus caused the curse of death that was pronounced in the garden to be reversed and broken off of humankind. He became a curse for us so that we might live (Galatians 3:13).

Unfortunately, there are many who have chosen to reject this good news. They subscribe to the theory that Jesus is not who the Bible says He was. In some cases, they say He is nothing but a mere man or prophet, but He's not the Savior. These people fail to realize that "in Him we have everything." He is the one-stop shop! Whatever we need can be found in Him, be it, joy, peace, satisfaction, life, health, strength, power, grace, love—the list goes on and on. Despite what our world around us has taught us, nothing can fulfill our desires and needs like Jesus can. Sadly, most people wait until their money, pride, health, strength, and joy have run dry until they run to the cross in need of a savior.

Living a life of total dependency on God is crucial. This is true no matter what phase of life you are in. Take for example the students enrolled in a college institution that is "preparing them for life." This means the information they gather here will most likely dictate the rest of their lives. This is a very daunting thought when you think about. An individual will spend over four years possibly being brainwashed and led outside of the will of God. This is not to say there is anything wrong with obtaining a college education. However, the point is that many will not pray or seek God before choosing an institution or major for a career. Obviously, the results can be devastating. An individual can potentially spend four years, thousands of dollars, and a lot of energy, only to discover that they had a calling that had nothing to do with their career.

One of the main reasons for this plot is the fact that we live in a society where we are encouraged from a young age to have a dream. This dream is essentially what we want to be when we grow up. We are told to find a role model to become like and pursue our dreams. The American dream is essentially get a college degree, start a family, buy a house with a white-picket fence, and retire early. We are conditioned to believe and adopt the formula: you plus your hard work equals success. But what does God have to say about this formula of success? According to Joshua 1:8, "Keep this Book of the Law always on your lips; meditate on it day and night, so that you may be careful to do everything written in it. Then you will be prosperous and successful" (NIV). Clearly, this is a contradiction to what the formula of the world says. Furthermore, Jesus taught the disciples, "Your kingdom come, your will be done" (Matthew 6:10 NIV). For individuals to be truly successful, they must adopt God's way of doing things. Every Christian must be mindful daily that we are part of a kingdom that operates independently of the world. We can't afford to allow the devil to trick us into doing the opposite. God's formula for success is you plus God's Word equals success.

From the beginning, the devil has always been a copycat. God spoke to Adam, and therefore the devil spoke to Eve. Everything that Satan does is a distorted version of what God has already done. The point I'm trying to make is no matter what offer Satan has placed on the table before you, it's only a sign that a better version has already been given to you by God! The devil comes to steal, kill, and destroy (John 10:10). God never intended for the devil to be able to tell us what to do, no less than a parent would allow a stranger to tell their children what to do. He is the father of lies, but not our heavenly Father. Therefore, he cannot—I repeat, cannot—tell us what to do. The next time the devil tries to tell you what to do, boldly declare, "You are not my Father!"

CHAPTER 4
Dominion

Then God said, let us make mankind in our image, in our likeness, so that they may rule over the fish in the sea and the birds in the sky, over the livestock and all the wild animals, and over all the creatures that move along the ground. So God created mankind in his own image, in the image of God he created them; male and female he created them. God blessed them and said to them, "Be fruitful and increase in number; fill the earth and subdue it. Rule over the fish in the sea and the birds in the sky and over every living creature that moves on the ground.

—Genesis 1:26–28 (NIV)

God's original intention for humankind was that we walk in authority and have rule and dominion (Genesis 1:26). God never intended for animals to have rule over humans. Nevertheless, we see in the garden how Eve subjected herself to the rule of a snake. This snake is also known as the "ancient serpent," otherwise known to most by the name of Satan. The devil could not wait to distort the image of God's prized possession, namely Adam and Eve. Prior to his fall from heaven, according to Ezekiel 28:12–19 he occupied the position of the anointed cherub (Ezekiel 28:14). He was adorned with every precious jewel one can imagine (Ezekiel 28:13). At the time, he was God's display of perfection, full of wisdom and perfect in beauty (Ezekiel 28:12b).

We can probably assume that Satan was the highest of all angels. He had enough persuasion to convince one-third of the angels to accompany him in a rebellion against God (Revelation 12:4). This resulted in Satan's fall from heaven. He was banished from the presence of God eternally as a result of his pride. He could not accept the fact that in the presence of God, he would be reduced to second best. He wanted to be God, stating, "I will ascend to the heavens; I will raise my throne above the stars of God; I will sit enthroned on the mount of assembly, on the utmost heights of Mount Zaphon" (Isaiah 14:13 NIV).

Once on Earth, Satan observed that this new creation of God bore His glory, which to Satan was a reminder that his previous position was forever lost. And now he had to stand aside and watch the glory of God manifest upon a human being, whom he knew was a lesser ranking being than he was in the order of creation. "You have made them a little lower than the angels and crowned them with glory and honor" (Psalm 8:5 NIV). Satan's primary mission henceforth became to cause humans to fall from glory and dominion as he did. Adam transferred all dominion and authority to Satan when he yielded to Satan's temptation to eat the forbidden fruit. The moment Adam and Eve exchanged the truth for a lie, they lost all the privileges of being in the garden of Eden.

Since the incident in the garden, humankind has been on a perpetual search for restoration back to Eden status. How is this the case? After all, you may be thinking to yourself, "I don't even like gardens, let alone desire to be in one." Before you dismiss this idea, please let me elaborate. The word *Eden* referenced in the book of Genesis means "pleasure" in its original form. That's right: God placed Adam and Eve in a garden of pleasure with eternity in mind. Isn't it wonderful to think that God did not want to hold back any good thing from His children, except for sin? God wanted us to have perpetual laughter, love, provision, protection, prosperity, good health, and most of all unlimited access to fellowship with Him. What could be better than that? No bowl of ice cream, shopping spree, or lavish bank account could ever compare to that. If you really think about it, God wanted us to have what He has: access to and rule over everything!

God never intended for us to lack anything. As a matter of fact, a brief study of the Bible will prove to us that God usually blesses us with more than we need. The Bible assures us that God can do for us exceedingly abundantly above all that we can ask or think (Ephesians 3:20). However, we must position ourselves in faith to receive all that God has in store for us. We must get back to a place in God where we believe Him to be our sustainer, maker, and provider.

The doubt that Satan introduced to Eve when he asked, did God really say, you must not eat from any tree in the garden? is one that still haunts us today. There are many individuals who reason, "Is God even real? Is heaven or hell real? Is Jesus truly the Son of God? Am I truly a child of God? Does God love me as much as John 3:16 suggests?" The answer to all the above is yes! We must be honest with ourselves and admit that we are currently struggling (or have in the past struggled) with exchanging the truth of God's Word for a lie sourced by Satan himself. If you still are not convinced that you are among those that fall into this category, let me give you some examples. Have you struggled:

1. To believe in yourself, your innate abilities, or your strengths?
2. To accept your human limitations, imperfections, flaws, or shortcoming?
3. To accept the image reflected when you look in the mirror?
4. To accept that you are lovable despite all of your mistakes?
5. To believe your future can be brighter than your dark past?

If you said yes to any of the above, then you have at some point exchanged the truth for a lie. But the good news is that Jesus Christ came on the Earth to restore all that Adam lost in garden of Eden. The scriptures tell us the first man, Adam, became a living person. But the last Adam—that is, Christ—is a life-giving Spirit (1 Corinthians 15:45). Romans 5:19 puts it even more clearly: "For just as through the disobedience of the one man the many were made sinners, so also through the obedience of the one man the many will be made righteous" (NIV). As the second Adam, Jesus was able to restore the fellowship, authority, and dominion lost by Adam in the garden.

Jesus's arrival on Earth was a clarion call from God to humankind to come back to Eden status. God never intended for humankind to experience any less than the privileges He allowed them in the garden: abundance, prosperity, eternal life, joy, peace, power, and an unlimited supply of His love. Jesus became the Way (back to God), the Truth (that would expose the lies of Satan) and the Life (eternal source of life) (John14:6).

From the very foundation of the Earth, Adam's relationship with God was reliant on his faith and obedience to God's Word. This was the governing principle in Adam's relationship to God in Eden. Adam was instructed by God once not to eat from the tree of knowledge of good and evil (Genesis 2:16–17). Adam was not created to die; death was an intrusion courtesy of Satan. Adam's willful disobedience resulted in paradise lost with the introduction of pain, suffering, and death. Scripture is abundantly clear that there was no death and suffering until after Adam's transgression.

Jesus Christ, the last Adam, freely offered Himself as atonement (i.e., the reconciliation of God and humankind through Jesus's sacrificial death on the cross) for the sin of humans, and He purchased eternal life for all who would trust in Him. Jesus's death paid the bill that Adam's sin incurred. Only the great Potter can repair broken pieces! As the Potter of our lives, He alone knows all the intricate details of our lives; no one is better equipped than God to tend to our needs. When Adam and Eve entered the garden, they lacked nothing. God provided for them everything that they needed in advance. God made provisions for their bodies (food, drink, and shelter), spirit (intimacy and fellowship with God), and soul (companionship in marriage).

In the same way, God has already made every necessary provision for your life. You may not be able to physically see them, but you can trust that by the love and grace of God, they are awaiting you. God has made plans to cover not only your sin with the blood of Jesus but also your needs by the grace of Jesus. He wants to restore to you everything that you lost and was stolen. No more walking around with your head hanging low. There is hope and life in Jesus. Every time potters put their hands to the wheel, they are unraveling a plan. In the same way, your life is being fashioned by the "wheel," better known as the will of God. Sit back and enjoy the ride as we discover through the pages of this book why you are indeed the Master's piece.

CHAPTER 5

The Reality of Two Realms

Before I formed you in the womb I knew
you, before you were born I set you apart;
I appointed you as a prophet to the nations.

—Jeremiah 1:5 (NIV)

Most people will not readily admit that they were created in the presence of God, assigned a destiny, and then given a body to enter the earth to fulfill their destiny. However, this is absolutely the case no matter how absurd it may seem. I realize this may be a hard concept to grasp because it is not common knowledge. Since the beginning of time, there have always been and will forever be two realms at play. God is Spirit, and as the Creator of all things, He existed before there was the Earth or humans to fill it. In Genesis 1, it states that darkness hovered over the Earth until the Spirit of God spoke light into existence. The principle here is that the spiritual governs the physical realm because God set it up that way. God's authority over the Earth was displayed in response to His commands. At His command came forth light, evening, morning, vegetation, living creatures, and more.

In the same way, God commanded Adam to have dominion over the earth and exercise it by speaking words. God created humans in His image: "So God created human beings in his own image. In the image of God he created them; male and female he created them" (Genesis 1:27 NIV). Then He gave them authority to operate in both the natural realm and the supernatural. Nevertheless, one major requirement to operate in this God-given authority is faith.

Faith, which is the substance of things hoped for and the evidence of things not seen (Hebrews 11:1), is the basic element of our walk with God. God is spirit and cannot be seen, so faith remains the key to accessing the supernatural and making it prevalent in the natural or physical realm. Furthermore, the Bible states that faith comes by hearing the Word of God (Romans 10:17). One of the most significant ways to build up our faith is by studying the Bible. In Joshua 1:8, Joshua was reminded that his success and prosperity would be directly related to his ability to retain and meditate upon the Word of God.

These scriptures are evidence of the fact that God has designed His Word as building agents for our faith. As we come into agreement with the Word of God, it becomes essential that we speak it as evidence of our belief. Paul declared in 2 Corinthians 4:13, "Having the same spirit of faith ... I believed, and therefore did I speak" (NIV).

Many people don't realize how powerful their words are. The reality is whatever we believe, we will speak. What we speak has the power to significantly shape our lives. Therefore as Christians, we must speak what God says, not what our circumstances or own thoughts say to us. If I am sick in my body, I must declare, "By His stripes I am healed" (Isaiah 53:5). If I am in lack, I must declare, "The Lord is my Shepherd, I shall not want" (Psalm 23:1). If I am faced with spiritual attacks, I must declare, "No weapon formed against me shall prosper" (Isaiah 54:17). The most powerful words that will ever affect your life will be the words you speak. "The tongue has the power of life and death, and those who love it will eat its fruit" (Proverbs 18:21 NIV). We must choose our words wisely. The Word of God is anointed with power to bring life to its hearers and recipients.

How do we live and walk in this power and authority? Paul alludes to the answer in his writings to the Corinthians when he mentioned that upon his arrival to see the believers there, he would expect nothing less but to see the demonstration of power in their lives. "For the kingdom of God is not a matter of talk but of power" (1 Corinthians 4:20 NIV). Authority is power that has been delegated. For example, a police officer who pulls over a car or arrests a criminal does so by the authority of the government, not his own physical power. In the same way, authority has been assigned to us by God to use against Satan, who seeks to steal, kill, and destroy God's blessing in our lives (John

10:10). The Bible gives us several scriptures that delineate this, some of which are as follows.

> I have given you authority to trample on snakes and scorpions and to overcome all the power of the enemy; nothing will harm you. (Luke 10:19 NIV)

> I will give you the keys of the kingdom of heaven; whatever you bind on earth will be bound in heaven, and whatever you loose on earth will be loosed in heaven. (Matthew 16:19 NIV)

> We demolish arguments and every pretension that sets itself up against the knowledge of God, and we take captive every thought to make it obedient to Christ. (2 Corinthians 10:5 NIV)

> God blessed them and said to them, be fruitful and increase in number; fill the earth and subdue it. Rule over the fish in the sea and the birds in the sky and over every living creature that moves on the ground. (Genesis 1:28 NIV)

When we understand the power and the authority that has been assigned to us by God, we will be more aggressive and less passive about spiritual opposition that we may face in our lives. As God's masterpiece, we have been fully equipped with all the necessary tools we need to live successful lives here on earth. God was very much aware that His children will have a devil to fight every now and then. Spiritual battles are very real whether or not we choose to admit it. In the Old Testament, the Israelites faced a myriad of physical enemies that were essentially being governed by their spiritual enemies. Every opposition they faced represented the forces of darkness that opposed their God and their faith. It was therefore important that God gave them key strategies to win every battle.

In Joshua 10, we find a story in which we see both forces at play: a war is about to take place between the Gibeonites and five other nations. However, we must first note that in chapter 9, it is revealed that the Gibeonites were a people who heard good things about Joshua and his army. They had heard of Joshua's undefeated status when it came to fighting battles. Under Joshua's leadership, the Israelites won every battle. Therefore, the Gibeonites feared Joshua's army and decided that if they couldn't beat them, they would join them. As chapter 9 progresses, we find out that the Gibeonites deceived Joshua into entering a covenant with them without God's approval. Hidden within the covenant Joshua made with the Gibeonites was a vow that their battles would be his battles and that under no circumstance would he harm them.

The Bible further reveals in chapter 9 that the only

reason Joshua entered this covenant with the Gibeonites was because he didn't seek the Lord through prayer for guidance. Although the Gibeonites' deceptive actions deserved death, because Joshua was a man of his word, he didn't kill them as promised. Nevertheless, he placed a curse on them that indefinitely made the Gibeonites servants of the children of Israel. In the beginning of chapter 10, five other kings representing distinct nations declared war on the Gibeonites when they were informed about the Gibeonites' alliance with Joshua. Although there was not a direct attack on Joshua, because of his covenant with the Gibeonites, he had to go to war as well.

It is essential for us to note when we make decisions outside of God's will, there will be great consequences awaiting us. Joshua was faced with an unnecessary battle that involved five nations, which meant opponents that were five times the size of his army. However, Joshua was a man of God who received favor from the Lord. God covered him because when God promises that He's with you, it is a promise that will never be broken. We see the result of God's faithfulness in Joshua 10:24. "When they had brought these kings to Joshua, he summoned all the men of Israel and said to the army commanders who had come with him, Come here and put your feet on the necks of these kings. So they came forward and placed their feet on their necks" (NIV).

How can we take what we've learned from Joshua and put it into practical use? First and foremost, your victory is compromised when you don't pray or seek the counsel of the Lord. As Christians, all our battles are likely to be spiritual in nature. This is due primarily to the fact that we are spiritual beings having a natural experience. Therefore, we must lean on spiritual strategies for victory, the number one strategy being taking instruction from our commander in chief!

Moreover, we must be mindful that we're living in between two realities, the spiritual and the natural. Be careful of people who come into your life unannounced because they usually have an agenda of their own. The Gibeonites unexpectedly came into Joshua's camp, and as a result, Joshua entered an unexpected war. These individuals are usually very flattering yet aggressive about getting to know you. The Gibeonites didn't genuinely want a relationship with Joshua, but rather what he had to offer. That is why you often find examples of individuals who are attracted to another because of their success. These same individuals will be likely to leave your life when you no longer have anything to offer because they simply wanted the things you had, not you.

In this season of our lives, God wants us to know that the devil can and will attack us through our relationships. Remember that Joshua's troubles were connected to his relationship with the Gibeonites. We must be prayerful about everyone whom we allow into our inner circles because we never know from where our next enemy is coming. The point is not for us to be paranoid, but we must be prayerful. These people include partners, church members, friends, family, coworkers, and more. That is why we must ask God to give us a spirit of discernment. "And no wonder, for Satan himself masquerades as an angel of light" (2 Corinthians 11:14 NIV).

Nevertheless, if you have been victimized in this matter already or have ignorantly allowed the enemy into your camp, please understand and walk in the authority that God has given you. Your past mistakes or your current circumstances do not define you, and neither can they keep you from the favor and forgiveness of God. In Joshua 10:13, Joshua goes from making a mess to making history. In Joshua 10:12–15, Joshua exercised his spiritual authority and commanded the sun and the moon to stand still as his enemies were completely destroyed.

> On the day the Lord gave the Amorites over to Israel, Joshua said to the Lord in the presence of Israel: sun, stand still over Gibeon, and you, moon, over the Valley of Aijalon. So the sun stood still, and the moon stopped, till the nation avenged itself of its enemies, as it is written in the Book of Jashar. The sun stopped in the middle of the sky and delayed going down about a full day. There has never been a day like it before or since, a day when the Lord listened to a human being. Surely the Lord was fighting for Israel! Then Joshua

returned with all Israel to the camp at Gilgal (NIV).

Furthermore, the five kings who went to hide in caves to avoid death were captured and executed. Upon their capture, Joshua commanded that his soldiers place their feet on the kings' necks prior to killing them, as a sign of utter defeat.

> When they had brought these kings to Joshua, he summoned all the men of Israel and said to the army commanders who had come with him, come here and put your feet on the necks of these kings. So, they came forward and placed their feet on their necks. Joshua said to them, do not be afraid; do not be discouraged. Be strong and courageous. This is what the Lord will do to all the enemies you are going to fight. (Joshua 10:24–25 NIV)

We must follow Joshua's example and do the same to every enemy of our souls. There are some kings in our lives that are in hiding, and we must capture and completely obliterate them: fear, low self-esteem, insecurity, doubt, double mindedness, impure thoughts, anger, bitterness, resentment, and unforgiveness. These "kings" have deceptively snuck into our lives with the intent to rule over us. For example, God may be calling us to let some things go, whereas fear is saying hold on to it because we need it to survive. If we're listening to fear, then we have made it our king. Whether we realize it or not, all of us have a king in hiding that we must capture. When you discover your opposing king, put your foot on its neck and kill it in Jesus's name!

CHAPTER 6
Faith Has Benefits

Have you been shipwrecked, hurt, bruised, abused, talked about, or mistreated? Have the events of your life ever left you wondering what could possibly be next? After all that you've been through, are you wondering whether you have anything left to give? If so, then this chapter is dedicated to you. It is my hope that you come to realize that despite the harsh dealings of life, you can still use what you have left. Most people, when they view the Bible, don't see it as a book containing real life stories to which they can relate. Most tend to assume that it is filled with sacred canonized writings that merely outline material for religious observance. Nevertheless, this approach is wrong and sadly overemphasized in society. On the contrary, I will prove through this chapter how relevant and relative the Bible is. We will look at the lives of a few people through which we may be able to see ourselves.

"Elisha replied to her, how can I help you?
Tell me, what do you have in your house?

Your servant has nothing there at all, she said, except a small jar of olive oil. Elisha said, go around and ask all your neighbors for empty jars. Don't ask for just a few. Then go inside and shut the door behind you and your sons. Pour oil into all the jars, and as each is filled, put it to one side. She left him and shut the door behind her and her sons. They brought the jars to her and she kept pouring. When all the jars were full, she said to her son, Bring me another one. But he replied, there is not a jar left. Then the oil stopped flowing. She went and told the man of God, and he said, go, sell the oil and pay your debts. You and your sons can live on what is left." (2 Kings 4:2–7 NIV)

The first story we will examine is derived from 2 Kings 4. In this story, we are introduced to a widow and her interaction with Elisha, who was a prophet at that time. This woman was in a very desperate situation: her husband had died and left her in debt. It was customary during this time that if people had a debt and could not pay, they had to offer themselves or their children as slaves to work until the debt was paid off. In this widow's case, her son's life was on the line—hence the alarming tone of the text.

After having explained her story to Elijah, he asks her a critical question: "What do you have in your house?" The only thing she owned that had any value was some oil, but it was almost gone. Elisha told the woman to collect empty jars from all her neighbors. She took her very small amount of oil and poured it into the first empty jar. Miraculously, the oil kept pouring until the jar was filled. She set it aside and poured oil into the next jar. One by one, she filled each jar until there were no empty jars left. The results were astounding: with this abundance of oil, the woman could sell the oil, pay her debt, and still have plenty of money left to provide for her needs and that of her son.

You may be wondering, "How does this widow's story relate to me? I'm not married, I have no kids, and I've never had an encounter with a prophet." Here's what I want you to consider with me just for a moment. The Lord took what little the woman had, and He multiplied it! I don't want you to focus so much on how or why He did what He did, but I need you to see what He did. It is crucial that we also unlock the symbolism in the text for a deeper understanding. The prophet in the story represents God. The widow's petition represents prayer. After all, what is prayer? It is merely a conversation with God that may or may not include a petition or supplication. Therefore, see yourself from the angle of taking a request to God in prayer.

Note that despite the absurdity of Elisha's response to her request, the widow followed suit. She did not debate the logic missing in the prophet's request. It would have been completely understandable for her to remind the prophet that this was her last meal. As a matter of fact, she could have reminded the prophet that her son would be the person who deserved the last meal. Nevertheless, she merely yielded to his requests. This required a great level of faith; why else would she risk the embarrassment of asking her neighbors for empty vessels? She expected a return on her investment to obey the prophet. You and I must realize that when we pray, we must believe that what we ask for by faith in Jesus, we will receive. The Bible assures us in Matthew 21:22, "If you believe, you will receive whatever you ask for in prayer" (NIV).

Why do we wrestle at times with our faith to believe God? What makes it so hard for us to take God at His word without needing a sign or another human being to affirm us? I suggest that there are several things that I like to refer to as faith blockers, which can quench our faith and put us at a disadvantage where we are not able to receive anything from God.

FAITH BLOCKERS

1. Words of Death

As believers, speaking words of life or positivity means that we are choosing to speak God's Word by faith, rather than the words evoked by our emotions based on current circumstances. The Bible reveals to us that the words that we speak will always fall into the categories of death or life. "The tongue has the power of life and death, and those who love it will eat its fruit" (Proverbs 18:21 NIV). This verse is a very powerful example of the relevance of believers choosing to speak what the Bible says instead of what we think or feel. Our thoughts often will not lend themselves to God's ways most of the times anyway (Isaiah 55:8–9). Therefore, we can't trust or rely on them to guide our choices daily. Our words reveal the contents of our hearts, which houses our belief system, which in turn shapes the daily events of our lives. In Genesis 1:3, God said let there be light, and light came forth. As a matter of fact, the Earth was filled with every living creature and aspect of nature because of God's verbal commands. God has endowed us with the same creative power to influence our environment with our words. Let's use it wisely!

2. Doubt

Just as courage is persisting in the face of fear, faith is persisting in the presence of doubt. Faith becomes a commitment, a practice, and a pact that is usually sustained by belief. Faith and doubt move in opposite directions and fight to cancel out each other. Whatever substance is stronger, we will see their results. Jesus rebuked the disciples in Matthew 17 because of their lack of faith. He told them that they needed faith as small as a mustard seed, and then nothing would be impossible for them. However, they let their doubt overpower their faith and rule the situation. It is possible to have both faith and doubt at the same time. So if all you need is faith as small as a mustard seed, then it is also true that your unbelief must be smaller than the amount of faith you possess to win. Believe God's promise to you. Don't look to the circumstance, only to the promise. Let faith swell on the inside of you, cancelling out all doubt.

3. Fear

Fear is an indicator that we either can't see God by faith or won't trust God. Fear will naturally breed unbelief that will put us at odds with God. The Bible states that without faith, it is impossible to please God (Hebrews 11:6), so we can safely say that fear blocks our ability to see, hear from, and ultimately receive from God. Unresolved fear will stunt our spiritual growth as well as obstruct our spiritual journey. The Christian's faith is a confident assurance in a God who loves us, knows our thoughts, and cares about our deepest needs. That faith continues to grow as we study the Bible and learn the attributes of His amazing character. The more we learn about God, the more we can see Him working in our lives and the stronger our faith grows.

These aforementioned faith blockers are just a few of many ideologies, habits, and traditions that interrupt the progress of faith in our lives. As we can see through the story of the widow, faith has benefits. As per the outcome of the widow's request, she became an entrepreneur overnight without any degree, money, or spousal support. Whatever you're running low on, be it strength, money, joy, peace, or ideas, I encourage you to take it to God in prayer by faith and watch Him multiply it to the degree that you can share it with others.

The next story that we are going to look at is found in John chapter 2 when Jesus and His disciples took time out to attend a wedding feast in the village of Cana with his mother. To understand the context of the story, it is important that we first review the history of that time. Jewish weddings were filled with tradition and ritual. One of the customs, much like today, was providing an extravagant feast for guests. Something went wrong at this wedding, however, because they ran out of wine early. In that culture, running out of wine was an occasion for great humiliation and ridicule on part of the bride and groom. Replenishing this wine was of the utmost importance and urgency.

Nearby were six stone jars filled with water that the Jews used for ceremonial cleansing of their hands, cups, and vessels before meals. Each large pot held twenty to thirty gallons. Jesus told the servants to fill the jars with water. He ordered them to draw some out and take it to the master of the banquet, who supervised food and drink. The master was unaware of Jesus's turning the water in the jars into wine; after all it was Mary, Jesus's mother, who'd brought the matter to Jesus to solve. The steward was amazed. He took the bride and groom aside and complimented them. Most couples served the best wine first, he said, and then brought out cheaper wine after the guests had too much to drink and would not notice. "You have saved the best till now, he told them" (John 2:10 NIV).

You may be wondering at this point, "How can I relate to this story? Once again, I'm not married, and neither have I been to a wedding where they ran out of wine." My question to you is, Have you ever been in a situation where your reputation and integrity were on the line? Have you ever had pressure to produce without adequate resources on hand? If so, then you can relate to the bride and groom in the story. Had they not invited Jesus to their wedding, the results may have been much different. Your faith in God and His Word will always be the difference between how your story began and how it will end. Faith has benefits. The greatest of them all will be to see the Master move on your behalf.

CHAPTER 7
It's an Inside Job

A fact that can be substantiated with much supporting evidence is that human beings by nature are self-centered rather than God-centered. "The mind governed by the flesh is hostile to God; it does not submit to God's law, nor can it do so" (Romans 8:7 NIV). Therefore, the sins that we commit daily without any help or coaching should be no surprise to us. It is crucial for us to understand our sinful nature for us to appreciate the gift of salvation through Christ. The Bible elaborates clearly on the works that we are inherently capable of producing left to our own devices: "The acts of the flesh are obvious: sexual immorality, impurity and debauchery; idolatry and witchcraft; hatred, discord, jealousy, fits of rage, selfish ambition, dissensions, factions and envy; drunkenness, orgies, and the like" (Galatians 5:19–21 NIV).

It is only by the grace of God and the Holy Spirit that we can produce any works that are worth mentioning and bring glory to God. "But the fruit of the Spirit is love, joy, peace, forbearance, kindness, goodness, faithfulness, gentleness and self-control. Against such things there is no law" (Galatians 5:22–23 NIV). Jesus made it clear that the key to our success in producing godly characteristics was staying connected to Him. "Remain in me, as I also remain in you. No branch can bear fruit by itself; it must remain in the vine. Neither can you bear fruit unless you remain in me. I am the vine; you are the branches. If you remain in me and I in you, you will bear much fruit; apart from me you can do nothing" (John 15:4–5 NIV). Unfortunately, we cannot undo our sinful nature; we can only give it to Jesus as our Savior to cover it by His blood. As we become more in tune with our sinful nature and our need for the Savior, we will notice the presence of an intricate part of our nature called the soul.

The soul is comprised of three compartments: mind, will, and emotions. Thoughts and feelings play an important role in our lives. As our feelings connect with our thoughts, emotions are formed. However, any traumatic experiences that occur in our lives has the potential to disrupt the internal processes that God has put in place. Emotional healing is something that every human being needs to one degree or another. At some point in our lives, we have been subject to emotional wounds. There are many variations of emotional brokenness and pain. Whether the cause is natural or it's because of another's sin or offense, we all fight some type of emotional battle. In Psalm 23, King David introduces us to God as the "restorer" of souls. Psalm 23:3 (NKJV) says, "He restores my soul." How can our souls be restored? The premise here is that God is the one at work in our lives. We cannot restore ourselves but must be restored by God. The literal translation for the phrase "He restores my soul" is "He causes my life to return." The word *restore* means to return to an original state and replenish. David wrote these words from experience as someone who endured brokenness and had to be repaired by God. From a young age, David had experienced rejection from his father and brothers. He knew from experience what it meant to be wounded in one's soul.

Rejection is one of the many grievous attacks on the soul that can leave an individual wounded beyond human repair. Studies have shown that rejection can lower our IQ, cause emotional pain, destabilize our need to belong, and create surges of anger or aggression. Rejection can manifest in a variety of ways. Typically, rejection has to do with an instance of a person or entity pushing something or someone away. A person may refuse to accept a gift, for example. In the field of mental health care, rejection most frequently refers to the feelings of shame, sadness, or grief people feel when they are not accepted by others.

An individual can even experience rejection after significant others end a relationship. A child who has few or no friends may feel rejected by peers. A person who was adopted may also experience feelings of rejection. Rejection can also result from life events not involving relationships, such as being turned down for a desired position at work or receiving a rejection letter from a college. Any rejection can be painful, but some instances of rejection may be more impactful than others. Because most humans desire social contact, and because many people crave acceptance from society, being rejected can incite negative feelings and emotions. But no rejection can trump that which we experience from family.

Like David, those of us who have experienced rejection on any level will come to know God as the restorer of our souls, if we are willing. As the manufacturer of our lives, God is the expert on how to fix anything that is broken. As a matter of fact, the Bible declares, "The Lord is close to the brokenhearted and saves those who are crushed in spirit" (Psalm 34:18). When sadness, grief, loneliness, or depression settles into one's mind, heart, and soul, it is not easy to dismiss these feelings. At times, inner despair remains despite any kind acts of others toward us. There are wounds that only God can heal. Contrary to popular belief, time does not heal all wounds—God does! If, like David, you are facing on a situation that has left your soul crying out for help, please realize that the healing of your soul is an inside job for God. Our God has made claims to not merely dwell among us but live inside of us.

> Jesus replied, "Anyone who loves me will obey my teaching. My Father will love them, and we will come to them and make our home with them." (John 14:23 NIV)

Do you not know that you are a temple of
God and that the Spirit of God dwells in you?
(1 Corinthians 3:16 NKJV)

I am crucified with Christ; and it is no longer
I who live, but it is Christ who lives in me.
(Galatians 2:20 NIV)

In Galatians 2:20, Paul did not say, "I live in a Christ-like way," or, "I glorify Christ through my behavior." No, he said, "Christ ... lives in me," clearly telling us that Christ lives in His believers. The Christian life is not a matter of merely behaving like Christ; rather, it is about allowing Christ Himself to live in and through us. As believers, we have twenty-four seven access to God as the Helper in our time of need because He lives within us.

This good news should be comforting to us and be the point at which our healing process begins. Whatever the internal conflict may be, whether emotional distress, mental conflict, or spiritual warfare, Jesus is the man for this inside job. Common problems like insecurity, anxiety, self-condemnation, or chronic fatigue may also be related to wounds or conflicts of the past from which we haven't healed. Even physical problems ranging from serious illnesses to common headaches may be caused in part by internalized stress and repressed emotion. How we respond to the painful situations of life is something we must pay close attention to.

Unfortunately, due to spiritual blindness, overindulgences in world practices many have resorted to more extreme measures of getting healing for the soul. From sexual perversion to chemical dependencies, addiction to modern technologies, and other self-help tactics, people have bypassed the grace of God and settled for the gadgets of this world. Although I am not opposed to technological advancements and other human resources to aide in our healing, we need to realize that all else outside of the love and power of God will inevitably fail us. Why settle for resources when you have the Source?

A generous application of God's Word to our lives each day would do wonders for restoring mental stability. This would eliminate the need for millions of pills, needles, cocktails, and psychiatrists. Health specialists assert that more hospital beds are occupied by those burdened with emotional problems than all physical and surgical ailments combined. Christ has the remedy for all problems that are not physiological in nature, and even when the sicknesses are physical, He can heal us or motivate us to endure by means of encouragement within the Word.

Mental and emotional healing was an aspect of Jesus's ministry that was declared at its onset: "He has anointed Me to preach the gospel to the poor; He has sent Me to heal the brokenhearted, to proclaim liberty to the captives and recovery of sight to the blind, to set at liberty those who are oppressed" (Luke 4:18 NKJV). Nevertheless, it is important to note that there is no quick and easy path to emotional healing. Some will say that all we need to do is accept Jesus, and we will be suddenly healed of our illnesses, emotional and otherwise. However, the truth is we are flesh-bound creatures who naturally resist the ways of the Spirit. Jesus said, "The spirit is willing, but the flesh is weak" (Matthew 26:41 NKJV). Acknowledging God as the restorer of our souls is honestly the first step to emotional healing. We must remember that healing is a process. It involves step-by-step, day-by-day choices to trust and obey the Lord.

Here are some practical things as followers of Christ we can do to find emotional healing.

1. Meditate on the Bible. God's instructions are "life to those who find them and health to one's whole body" (Proverbs 4:22).
2. Confess any known sins to God. "If we confess our sins, he is faithful and just and will forgive us our sins and purify us from all unrighteousness" (1 John 1:9).
3. Take control of our thought life. In the Spirit, "we take captive every thought to make it obedient to Christ" (2 Corinthians 10:5).
4. Abstain from old sinful habits. "We know that our old self was crucified with him so that the body ruled by sin might be done away with, that we should no longer be slaves to sin" (Romans 6:6). You have been called to holiness and to walk in newness of life (Romans 6:4).
5. Forgive those who have hurt you. This is important. "Be kind and compassionate to one another,

forgiving each other, just as in Christ God forgave you" (Ephesians 4:32). Be cautious of any root of bitterness in the soul (Hebrews 12:15).

6. See yourself as God sees you: loved (Romans 5:8), gifted (2 Timothy 1:7), set free (John 8:36), and washed, sanctified, and justified (1 Corinthians 6:11).

7. Get involved in a Bible-teaching local church. God gives spiritual gifts to His church "to equip his people for works of service, so that the body of Christ may be built up" (Ephesians 4:12). Part of a church's function is to aid the healing process of those who are emotionally or spiritually wounded.

Jesus Christ can help us find emotional healing without a doubt. When we have His Spirit dwelling within us, He can and will delight to transform us into the kind of people who are filled with love, power, and every positive emotion. All negative emotions and painful memories will have to flee at the sound of His name and power of His presence. He is more than your Savior; He is your Maker and Healer. Make an appointment with Him. Listen carefully to Him. Resolve to take the remedy He prescribes and then watch your soul prosper. He is the only man for this inside job!

CHAPTER 8
Divine Appointment

When you entered the Earth on the day you were born, at the exact time you were born, the countdown began on your life. The appointed time (Hebrews 9:27) that you were given is the frame of time to which I am referring. We all have been assigned a specific amount time related to a specific purpose on the Earth. This is true, regardless of the conditions of your birth: rich, poor, middle class, orphan, sick, healthy. Many people allow the conditions of their birth to define their self-worth or control their path to destiny. However, this couldn't be further from the truth. If we want to see a clear depiction of someone whose conditions at birth completely opposed His divine purpose, let's look at Jesus.

> And she brought forth her firstborn son, and wrapped him in swaddling clothes, and laid him in a manger; because there was no room for them in the inn. (Luke 2:7 NKJV)

The Bible makes known to us that when Jesus was born, His mother Mary laid Him in a manger. Traditionally, a manger was used as a feeding trough or storage for hay. Mangers were typically placed wherever livestock were kept, usually in stables or caves. One can only imagine the condition of this manger: animal droppings, hay fibers, and atrocious smells. I am sure you see where I am going with this. In ancient times and even today, this must be one of the most degrading places to ever lay a newborn child. However, when Mary and Joseph arrived in Bethlehem, there was no lodging available to them outside of the manger. Once they laid Jesus there, an angel told a group of nearby shepherds that they would find their newborn Messiah (i.e., Savior) and Lord "lying in a manger" (Luke 2:12 NKJV). Jesus was not laid in that manger by accident. As a matter of fact, it was assigned to Him by His heavenly Father. Furthermore, all the conditions surrounding Jesus's birth were prophetic.

The manger itself had a major spiritual significance. As already delineated, it was a "feeding place" for animals. The parallel here is that as animals go to mangers for physical food, so can we go to Jesus for spiritual food. As a matter of fact, He identified Himself as the Bread of Life (John 6:35) and the water that would cause us to never thirst again (John 4:14). Regardless of the repulsive location of Jesus's birth, His first bed was an indicator of His nature and purpose. I am sure there are many who feel He should've have come to earth amid fanfare and luxurious surroundings. However, the King of kings was born among animals, with His very first visitors being lowly shepherds. These shepherds were also symbolic in the sense that Jesus was the "Good Shepherd" who came to shepherd the souls of humankind. This humble king would grow up and attain the most prominent position ever to exist, which was by His Father's side in power and glory.

> "Nazareth! Can anything good come from there?" Nathanael asked. "Come and see," said Philip. (John 1:46 NIV)

According to historians, Nazareth was an insignificant village that gained its popularity mainly from the fact that it was the place where Jesus grew up and where his family lived. The city of Nazareth was a small and insignificant agricultural village in the time of Jesus. It had no trade routes, was of little economic importance, and was never mentioned in the Old Testament or other ancient texts. Consequently, Nathanael's question, which alluded to the fact that Nazareth could not produce anything worth mentioning, was legitimate.

Nathanael spoke a fact, not an opinion; he had every reason to doubt that there would be an exception to Nazareth's track record of irrelevance. Nathanael's reaction is a perfect example of how easy it is to fall prey to false judgments about people based on our personal biases. We must be careful not to be critical in our attitudes toward others without fully examining circumstances, merits, and character. If we were to strictly judge everyone solely by their place of origin, we would have easily rejected Jesus as Christ, confident in our misguided conception that no good thing could come out of Nazareth.

Unfortunately for Jesus, many of His fellow countrymen judged Him harshly and rejected His ministry. Their deep belief that nothing good could come out of Nazareth blinded them to the fact that God was in their midst through the person of Jesus. This was clearly indicated in Matthew 13:58, which states that Jesus did not do many mighty works there because of their unbelief while in Nazareth. Jesus was limited by their unbelief, which was prophetically written in the Old Testament as the people of Israel limited the Holy One of Israel through their unbelief (Psalm 78:41).

The lack of faith found in the hearts of the Nazarene kept them from fully experiencing the power, miracles, love, joy, and fellowship of God resident in Christ. I wonder how much of God we have missed the opportunity to experience through godly men and women due to our poor judgment of them. I must admit that there have been numerous times where I almost missed a blessing or a word from God due to the appearance, background, or social rank of an individual. Furthermore, I'm eager to know how many times you have felt ostracized, judged, or mislabeled by others. I can imagine if this is your plot, it doesn't feel too good.

I want to encourage and remind you that although the rash opinions of others may be based on facts, you don't have to allow yourself to be engulfed in them. Perhaps you came from a background of poverty, abuse, disdain, and the like. This in no way defines who you are or your destiny. However unfortunate the fact that many from His hometown did not believe in Jesus, it did not change the fact that He was sent by God. His mission was to save the world from their sins. As stated in Luke 19:10, "For the Son of Man came to seek and to save the lost" (NIV). Jesus's life is a prime example of the fact that your story does not determine your glory. His infamous hometown, bloodline, and childhood in no way impacted the fact that He was the Son of God who now sits at the right hand of the Father.

> "God raised Christ from the dead and seated
> him at his right hand in the heavenly places ...
> He put all things under his feet and gave him
> as head over all things to the church, which
> is his body, the fullness of him who fills all in
> all." (Ephesians 1:20–23 ESV)

If you have ever wondered how the negative circumstances of your life could ever amount to any real significance, I hope the story of Jesus answered the question for you. The reality is that as He revealed to the young prophet Jeremiah (Jeremiah 1:5), God knew you before you were even born. He assigned your life a purpose and then allowed you to enter the earth to fulfill it. The problem is that we have not been taught this in our schools, homes, or churches enough to believe it.

> "But why did you need to search?" he asked. "Didn't you know that I must be about my Father's business?" (Luke 2:49 NLV)

Jesus made this statement at the young age of twelve years old. It was during this time his parents (Mary and Joseph) were frantically looking for Him. Every year, it was the custom for Jesus's parents to go to Jerusalem for the Festival of the Passover. At this time, when the festival was over and his parents were returning home, Jesus stayed behind in Jerusalem, but they were unaware of it. Thinking He was in their company, they traveled on for a day. Shortly after, they began looking for Him among their relatives and friends. When they did not find Him, they went back to Jerusalem to look for Him. After three days, they found Him in the temple courts, sitting among the teachers, listening to them, and asking them questions. The Bible records that everyone who heard Him was amazed at His understanding and His answers (Luke 2:47).

Many people today are wearing bracelets with the letters WWJD, which means "What would Jesus do?" It's an important question. In finding the answer, the best source of information are the words of Jesus Himself. Jesus's words spoken in temple were His very first recorded in the Bible. His first words revealed His identity as the Son of

God. These words tell us a lot about Jesus and ultimately challenge us to be like Him. One of the first observations we can make is that Jesus speaks from a point of view of divinity. His words depict a sense of authority, freedom, and independence that contradict what an average twelve-year-old would be expected to have. The boy Jesus knew who He was and what He was called to do at a very young age. This is a good place to point out that with God, age is just a number, not an obstacle! There are no limits to whom God can use for any particular task in His service. Be mindful of this the next time you hear Him calling you. You are perfect for the job! As a matter of fact, you were born to do it.

The presence of Jesus on Earth was not an accident. He came to fulfill a specific plan and destiny for His life. Throughout His time on Earth, everything He did was in harmony with that plan. Jesus declared that He "must" be doing what He was doing. He had the inner sense of compulsion born of the Spirit of God; there was a sense of destiny about it. In Luke's gospel, we note the following.

- "Jesus must preach. But he said, I must proclaim the good news of the kingdom of God to the other towns also, because that is why I was sent." (Luke 4:43 NIV)

- "Jesus must suffer. And he said, The Son of Man must suffer many things and be rejected by the elders, the chief priests and the teachers of the law, and he must be killed and on the third day be raised to life.'" (Luke 9:22 NIV)

- "Jesus must be delivered up, be crucified, and rise again. The Son of Man must be delivered over to the hands of sinners, be crucified and on the third day be raised again." (Luke 24:7 NIV)

- "Must fulfill every prophetic word. He said to them, this is what I told you while I was still with you: Everything must be fulfilled that is written about me in the Law of Moses, the Prophets and the Psalms." (Luke 24:44 NIV)

Just like Jesus, we must know and be able to declare our mission here on Earth. Each of us was created by God with a specific purpose in mind (Ephesians 1:11), much like a potter who intentionally molds a piece of clay. I have highlighted enough biblical passages to support the fact that God appointed us a purpose long before we entered the earth in human form. The question is, How do we discover this destiny to fulfill it? We are not born with this knowledge, so it is something that is revealed to us along our Christian journey. There must first be a cohesion of our human nature with our spiritual nature. Because God is the one who holds all the knowledge pertaining to our lives past, present, and future, it is impossible to access this information outside of a relationship with Him. The problem is that many people today are turning to failing resources to discover who they are instead of God. There is no better way for us to come into total discovery of our purpose than to align ourselves with the Creator. God wants a relationship with us more than we can imagine. He wants to reveal to us hidden mysteries, loving promises, and our divine appointments.

CHAPTER 9
We Are His Masterpiece

For we are God's masterpiece. He has created
us anew in Christ Jesus, so we can do the
good things he planned for us long ago.
—Ephesians 2:10 (NLV)

According to the above scripture, God has custom-designed a unique plan for all those who have decided to put their trust in Jesus Christ. God selected you and me and chose us so "that in the ages to come He might show the exceeding riches of His grace in His kindness toward us in Christ Jesus" (Ephesians 2:7 KJV). We are God's masterpiece, His poem, His work of art. When we look at ourselves this way, we begin to understand our incredible value in Christ. One definition of the word *masterpiece* is "the perfect example of skill or excellence of any kind." What an amazing thing to consider! The redemptive work God does in us is the ultimate example of His excellence! Therefore no matter how we feel about ourselves, the fact is that in God's eyes, we hold precious eternal value.

The reality is when Jesus died on the cross, it wasn't merely an act of love; it was also an act of grace. His thought process was, *I'm going to recreate you into something beautiful, splendid, and magnificent. I'm the Artist; you're the art. I'm the Painter; you're the canvas. I'm the Sculptor; you're the marble. It doesn't matter what you looked like when I found you because when I am done making you over, people will not see you as they once knew you.* Jesus is an Artist, and you and I are His crowning achievement, His masterpiece! Like a beautiful poem, He has put great thought into the rhyme and rhythm of our lives. When our heavenly Father looks at us, all He sees is beauty and greatness. God does not care about the negative things that others have to say about us, and neither should we. Unfortunately, we are living in a time when most people are bound by the likes, opinions, and affirmations of others.

Have you or any loved one ever questioned your worth? Low self-esteem is entirely based on what you believe about yourself. Unfortunately, the negative messages received from a parent, friend, spouse, or any significant person in our lives may cause us to feel worthless. No matter the cause for our low self-esteem, God does not promote or support this state of mind. He places great value on us. In fact, He sent His Son, Jesus, to die for our sins because of His desire to draw us closer to Him and make us part of His family (John 3:16). Our worth is so high that it cost Jesus His blood.

Everyone lacks confidence occasionally, but those encumbered with low self-esteem feel unhappy or unsatisfied with themselves most of the time. Low self-esteem, if left unresolved, can become an actual thinking disorder in which an individual will view themselves as inadequate, unworthy, unlovable, or incompetent. This negative self-view will then permeate every thought, leading to faulty assumptions and ongoing, self-defeating behavior.

Typically, people with low self-esteem

- are extremely critical of themselves;
- downplay or ignore their positive qualities;
- judge themselves to be inferior to their peers;
- don't believe a person who compliments them;
- use negative words to describe themselves, such as stupid, fat, ugly, or unlovable; and
- blame themselves when things go wrong.

For many, the eagerness to constantly please others stems from low self-esteem. Their thought process is that if they say yes to everything asked of them, they will somehow be accepted and liked. Furthermore, many people-pleasers confuse pleasing people for kindness. Consequently, they allow others to take advantage of them because of a reluctance to say no. What more validation can a person want than to have the approval, love, forgiveness, and inheritance of our Lord Jesus Christ? There is no greater love that can affirm us than the love expressed for us on the cross at Calvary. "Greater love has no one than this: to lay down one's life for one's friends" (John15:13 NIV).

For this reason, Christ must take preeminence in our lives. Jesus Christ is the Way, the Truth, and the Life (John 14:6). What He says is true regardless of what anyone else says or does, no matter how many contrary thoughts are assaulting your brain. As we grow in our understanding of who we are in Christ, we can easily let go of wrong thinking or any rejection from others. When we believe how precious we are in God's sight, our actions will follow suit.

IMAGE IS EVERYTHING

> Then God said, "Let us make mankind in our image, in our likeness, so that they may rule over the fish in the sea and the birds in the sky, over the livestock and all the wild animals, and over all the creatures that move along the ground." (Genesis 1:26 NIV)

In 1989 tennis player Andre Agassi became famous for a slogan that went viral: "Image is everything." We live in a society where we are bombarded daily with media advertisements that feature beautiful models, adorable puppies, cute babies, and more. Research studies suggest that we make brand purchase decisions based on the associations and feelings as opposed to the facts and statistics. We are essentially being conditioned to purchase products and adjust our lives according to an image. Image is undeniably threaded into most of our daily decisions of what to wear, what to purchase, and with whom to affiliate.

Most individuals do not see a reflection of God their Creator in themselves. As a matter of fact, most people are not willing to admit that the Creator exists. They would much rather settle for the lie that we are derivatives of evolution or a big bang. However, those of us who have read the book of Genesis can attest that these individuals are sadly mistaken. The truth is we have all, both male and female, been made in the image of the eternal Father who loved us enough to send us His Son, Jesus, so that we could have tangible evidence of this love. The next time you look in the mirror, ask yourself, What do you see? Are you a product of the opinions of others or the revelatory truth that you were made in the image of God? Perhaps you have been looking for your identity in the approval of others. Maybe you've been looking for it in your performance and role at work or at home. Today is the day that you can transition from finding your identity in what you do to finding out who you are in Christ.

TRUTH ABOUT OUR NEW IDENTITY IN CHRIST

1. You are now a child of God and part of God's family (John 1:12).
2. You are a new creation in Christ. The old has gone; the new has come (2 Corinthians 5:17).

3. You have been justified by faith in Christ and have peace with God ... Thus, you no longer must work to try to make yourself right before God (Romans 5:1).
4. You have been completely forgiven through faith in Christ and His death and resurrection (Ephesians 1:7).
5. You are completely loved by God in Christ (Romans 5:8; John 17:23; John 3:16).
6. You are "in Christ" (John 17:21; Colossians 3:3).
7. You are on your way to heaven (John 3:16; John 3:36).
8. Nothing can separate you from the love of Christ (Romans 8:35–39).
9. The Holy Spirit now indwells you forever (John 14:16; Ephesians 1:14).

The steadfast love of the Lord never ceases;
His mercies never come to an end; they are
new every morning; great is your faithfulness.
(Lamentations 3:22–23 ESV)

A New Year's resolution traditionally has been defined as a position in which a person makes the decision to change an undesired trait or behavior by setting and working toward personal goals of improvement. Research studies suggest that 35 percent of individuals who make New Year's resolutions break them by the end of January. Furthermore, it has been said that only 23 percent of those who make a resolution will see it through to completion. What can be said about these astounding statistics? Old habits die hard ... especially bad habits. Nevertheless, New Year's resolutions, as fickle as they may be at times, present a big opportunity for self-improvement.

There is something exciting about the beginning of a new year or season that can make people feel as though they are being offered a fresh start. On New Year's, most have a tendency to look back on past failures with an optimistic urge and desire to change. But my goal today is to suggest to you a new way of looking at resolutions for the new year. The Bible informs us in the above scriptures that God's mercy is renewed every morning. This means that every day we see is filled with newness and fresh opportunity to do things better than the day before. The grace offered to us daily by God is intended to do just that: make us better! However, like most opportunities, this grace will do us no good unless we accept it and make the best of it. For example, lemons are available to us daily, but only those who make lemonade would have seized an opportunity.

The reality is your new year can begin today or tomorrow or the day after that. You can resolve in your mind that you don't need a New Year's celebration to focus on a new you. Rather, you can choose to put one foot in front of the other daily as you grasp the mercy of God and become better today than the day before. God loves us enough to allow us a fresh start daily in life. A new mind equals a new you; a new day equals a new year. May your new year begin today as the new you fully embraces the grace of God to never be the same. You are His masterpiece created anew in Christ Jesus. Embrace it and be forever changed.

CHAPTER 10
No Looking Back

Then the LORD said to Joshua, today I have
rolled away the reproach of Egypt from you.

—Joshua 5:9 (NIV)

A reproach is a condition caused by shame, discredit, or disgrace. For all intents and purposes, reproach can take on many forms. Throughout the Bible, we saw that it happened via sexual abuse (2 Samuel 3:13), barrenness (Genesis 30:23), widowhood (Isaiah 54:4), hunger (Ezekiel 36:30), disease (Job 19:5), uncircumcision (Genesis 34:14; Joshua 5:9), or injuries from enemies (Nehemiah 1:3). Perhaps there are some things on the above list to which you can relate. Perhaps there are things that you went through that are not listed, but you can identify with the sentiment associated with reproach by all the above. If so, I want to encourage you by informing you that although you may be haunted by a past filled with pain, tragedy, or remorse, God can help you overcome every ounce of reproach from the past. Furthermore, God doesn't view us in relation to what happened to us; He is more concerned by what He does in us.

Although God is loving, forgets our past, and does not hold it against us, we have an adversary, Satan, who likes to resurrect the past to inflict a sense of shame and worthlessness on us. Today, the good news that I have for you is that the Lord can and will remove the reproach from your past.

Forget the former things; do not dwell on the past. See, I am doing a new thing! Now it springs up; do you not perceive it? I am making a way in the wilderness and streams in the wasteland. (Isaiah 43:18–19 NIV)

I am leaving this place now,
letting go of all my fears,
saying goodbye to the memory I hold dear
I can finally breathe again,
it's a new day fair well past,
as I close this chapter I set free at last
I made up my mind-there's no turning back
the past is behind me-there's no looking back
I'm looking forward not behind
I've made a decision-to give you my life
and there's no looking back ...

The previous words are lyrics to one of my favorite gospel songs, "No Looking Back" by Damita Haddon. This song was a fresh reminder of the resolve that I made since the age of fifteen years old to commit my life to Christ. The lyrics, much like the Bible passage before it, inspired me to move forward beyond the horrors of my past and into the brightness of my future. As the saying goes, no one can drive forward looking in the rearview mirror. From offenses to failures to trauma, we must find the strength within us to let them go! It's almost as if I can hear God speaking to our past as He did to Pharaoh in Egypt, saying, "Let my people go."

As was the case during that biblical era, God has plans for us beyond the former bondage of our past that will blow our minds, if we cooperate enough to receive them. There are so many people today enduring severe mental, spiritual, and in some cases physical anguish because of their inability to let go of the past. In this new, approaching season of your life, you cannot afford to be like the Israelites, who were so bound to their past that they couldn't enjoy the freedom of their present enough to walk into their promising future. What a tragedy it would be to miss out on the best God has for you due to your inability to believe that better days are ahead of you. Despondency, self-pity, doubt, unforgiveness, and fear are things that can hinder us from entering our Promised Land.

While living as slaves in Egypt, the Israelites were treated with great cruelty for many years (Exodus 1:11–14). They were beaten down physically, mentally, and emotionally. As slaves, they were forced to believe that they had no worth, couldn't do anything right, and would never measure up. Over time, this led them to suffer from low self-esteem, insecurity, and a loss of identity. This is almost always the case when a person is being mistreated or abused for any amount of time. As a result, instead of acknowledging the perpetrator doing them wrong, victims of abuse tend to accept the blame and start accepting the abuse as something they deserve or caused to happen. Before long, shame and reproach will settle in, leading the individual to spiral downward if not helped.

The 430 years the Israelites spent in slavery was indeed a significant amount of time. But just as God promised He would, He delivered them out of the slavery and abuse. Furthermore, right when they were about to enter the Promised Land, God said to them, "This day I have rolled away the reproach of Egypt off of you" (Joshua 5:9 NIV). Notice that they couldn't go into the Promised Land with the feelings of shame and unworthiness. God had to roll away the reproach, which haunted them long after the slavery ended. In the same way, before you and I can reach our highest potential, we must be free of all reproach associated with our past. Despite our mistakes or the injustices of others toward us, we cannot afford to sit around feeling guilty or condemned, blaming ourselves or others. Whatever painful experience you're coming out of, whether it be a divorce, an abusive relationship, an addiction, or somebody who wrongfully hurt you, God is offering you today to roll away the reproach.

He's rolling away the guilt and the shame. Now it's up to you to accept it. You must quit dwelling on your failures. Quit repeating the painful experiences in your mind. Quit believing the lie that you've made too many mistakes or have been hurt too badly to love again. Just as He did for the Israelites, so will He do for you. God is the same yesterday, today, and forever (Hebrews 13:8). At the next encounter you have with those evil voices reminding you of your shameful past, you must answer right back and declare, "My reproach has been taken away in Jesus's name!"

The reality is that God has so much more in store for us beyond the promise of eternity in heaven. He desires for us to have abundant, fruitful, and purposeful lives here on earth—lives filled with peace and prosperity that we could never achieve on our own human efforts. The condition to this blessing, however, is to believe God enough to make daily strives toward the future without entertaining the interruption of a corrupt past. God is offering us today an opportunity to move forward, step out on faith, and receive His best for our lives. You and I can do this only after we have resolved to let go of it, whatever *it* is.

I am not suggesting this will be easy, but it is vital to the outcome of our future. Better days are ahead of us, and the worst is behind us. Let's make a resolution today to move forward into a new season, era, and chapter of our lives. God is not only with us, but as can be seen in the story of the Israelites in the wilderness, He goes before us and has our backs (Exodus 13:21). We have nothing to fear but so much to gain by letting go of yesterday and embracing today while looking forward to a brighter, more promising tomorrow.

CROSSING OVER

> Remember the command that Moses the servant of the Lord gave you after he said, The Lord your God will give you rest by giving you this land ... but all of your fighting men, ready for battle, must cross over ahead ... until they have taken possession of the land the Lord your God is giving them. (Joshua 1:13–15 NIV)

As indicated in the above passage, prior to the death of Moses, the Israelites were given all the land east of the Jordan by Moses. Before we delve any further into the scripture, we must discuss the background of this chapter and book of the Bible. I'd like to first bring to your attention the title of this book, Joshua, which means "Yahweh saves." Consequently, central to the theme of this book in the Bible is God saving His people by conquering their enemies and distributing among the Israelites their promised homeland, Canaan. This promise could be traced back to Abraham's covenant with God: "I will make you into a great nation, and I will bless you; I will make your name great, and you will be a blessing, I will bless those who bless you, and whoever curses you I will curse; and all people on earth will be blessed through you" (Genesis 12:2–3 NIV). The Lord essentially made a contract with Abraham promising him the unconditional blessings of receiving land, posterity, and spiritual blessings. Thus, the book of Joshua records the fulfillment of Abraham's promise received centuries prior.

Now that we have a better understanding of the background of the text, we can appreciate the command given by God to Joshua to get ready to cross the Jordan River into a land He was about to give to the Israelites. The people had now reached a place I'd like to refer to as a crossroad. While under the leadership of Moses, they received and dwelled in the land east of the Jordan River. The only thing that stood between them and the Promised Land was the body of water. This obstacle was similar to one that they had previously faced while under the leadership of Moses— the Red Sea experience.

The Israelites had encountered the obstacle of the Red Sea while they were fleeing the presence of Pharaoh and his army and seeking a refuge from slavery. While at the Red Sea, God commanded Moses to extend his rod over the water to initiate the parting of it. Once parted, the dry land of the Red Sea became a road of victory for the Israelites as they crossed over toward the direction of the awaited Promised Land. Unfortunately for Pharaoh and his army, who attempted to pursue them during their deliverance, the dry land of the parted sea became a place of doom for the enemies of the Israelites.

This is a good place to remind you that on your road to victory, there will be obstacles to overcome, however with God as your guide, you are sure to overcome each one with grace and ease. The one thing that most times we fail to keep in mind is that God is not so much interested in the fears, panic, or anxiety we are experiencing while at our crossroads in life. He is more interested in our ability to see our difficult circumstances as platforms or opportunities for Him to show Himself strong in our lives and display His power and glory. He is fully aware of our lack of strength, resources, and power. However, He is looking to see whether we acknowledge His strength, resources, and power, which are readily available to us by faith. Overcoming our past is by far the most difficult part of a new beginning. If we are not careful harboring guilt and shame can enslave us to further guilt and shame through self-hatred and self-rejection. This is precisely why God rolling away our reproach is such an important prerequisite to obtaining all the promises that God has in store for us. If I had not developed the courage and the faith to let go of my past and embrace the love of God and the newness of each day, I would have never known that my Master can take my mess and turn it into a message. You are reading this book today because of the grace allotted to me to be my Master's piece!

ABOUT THE AUTHOR

Precious Gem was born in Brooklyn, New York, and has encountered many hardships in her life. Despite her trials, she retained her love and passion for God and bears the burden of spreading the love of Jesus Christ through teaching and writing. She currently lives with her husband and son in Massachusetts.